The Infinite Potential of Women

An Address by Her Holiness
Sri Mata Amritanandamayi Devi

Delivered at the 2008 Summit of the
Global Peace Initiative of Women:
"Making Way for the Feminine:
For the Benefit of the World Community"

Jaipur, Rajasthan, India — March 7th 2008

Translated by Swami Amritaswarupananda Puri

The Infinite Potential of Women

Translated by Swami Amritaswarupananda Puri

Published by
 Mata Amritanandamayi Mission Trust
 Amritapuri P.O., Kollam Dt.,
 Kerala 690 525, India
 E-mail: info@theammashop.org
 Website: www.amritapuri.org
 www.embracingtheworld.org

Copyright © 2008 by Mata Amritanandamayi Mission Trust

All rights reserved. No part of this publication may be stored in a retrieval system, transmitted, reproduced, transcribed or translated into any language, in any form, by any means without the prior agreement and written permission of the publisher.

First Edition: April 2008, 4000 copies
Second printing: June 2009, 1500 copies
Third printing: June 2010, 2000 copies
Fourth printing: June 2013

Amma and Dena Merriam, convenor of the Global Peace Initiative of Women, during the summit's invocation prayer.

The Global Peace Initiative of Women's 2008 Summit brought together several hundred people to discuss how feminine leadership could transform religion, politics, economics and society in general. It was an eclectic gathering, drawing both religious and spiritual heads, policy-makers, academics and educators, healthcare professionals and human-rights activists.

Introduction

The Global Peace Initiative of Women's 2008 summit, "Making Way for the Feminine: for the Benefit of the World Community," brought together several hundred people to discuss how feminine leadership could transform religion, politics, economics and society in general. It was an eclectic gathering, drawing both religious and spiritual heads, policy-makers, academics and educators, healthcare professionals and human-rights activists, as well as a couple dozen young people from countries of conflict.

The summit took place at the Clarks Amer Hotel in Jaipur, the capital of Rajasthan, in northern India, from March 6 – 10, corresponding with Amma's annual *darshan* program in the Pink City. On March 7, Amma delivered a heartfelt and impassioned speech titled "The Infinite Potential of Women," that focused on the oppression of women in various sectors of society.

In many ways, the address was an extension of the landmark speech Amma delivered at the

The Infinite Potential of Women

Global Peace Initiative of Women's first summit, at the headquarters of the United Nations in Geneva in 2002, "The Awakening of Universal Motherhood."

In 2002, Amma extolled the immense power of feminine energy, and said that, for the good of the world, it was imperative for women to join men at the forefront of society. In this regard, Amma asked women to believe in themselves, and men to not only stop blocking women's ascent, but to assist it. What made Amma's vision unique was her insistence that women should not rise as imitation men, but through fully embracing and nurturing their innate motherliness. Amma said that the fibre of a women's existence was her motherly love, compassion, patience and selflessness, and that she should never abandon these qualities at any cost. If women reject their feminine qualities, Amma said, it would only add to the imbalance currently being experienced in the world. "The forthcoming age should be dedicated to re-awakening the healing power of motherhood," Amma said. "This is the only way to realize our dream of peace and harmony for all."

Introduction

In her 2008 speech in Jaipur, Amma continually lamented the deterioration of love and mutual respect between men and women and, for the sake of world peace and harmony, urged their repair. "Women and men should join hands to save our society and the coming generations from a huge disaster," Amma said. "Instead, the situation today is akin to two heavily loaded vehicles speeding towards each other from opposite directions, each unprepared to move aside to let the other pass."

Furthermore: "If the future is to be a beautiful, fragrant, fully blossomed flower, women and men must join hands in all spheres. Those who desire peace and contentment in the world community must pay heed to this, right now, in this very moment. For the sake of a promising future, the minds and intellects of women and men need to become one. We cannot wait any longer. The more we delay, the worse the state of affairs in the world will become."

Amma also focused on specifics, going into great detail about various ways women are being oppressed and exploited—specifically addressing the problems of prostitution, rape, Internet pornography, the dowry system, divorce and female infanticide.

Amma also reiterated ideas expressed in her 2002 address, continuing to stress the importance of women rooting their lives in the qualities associated with motherhood and seeking not external but internal equality. "Everything has its own essential nature…," Amma said. "Light is the nature of the sun, waves the nature of the sea and coolness the nature of wind. What endows a deer with placidity and a lion with cruelty are their own original natures. Similarly, women and men have their own unique natures that distinguish them from each other. These should be remembered and never abandoned."

Amma concluded by addressing women directly: "Women already hold everything they need to shine forth in society. She is faultless. She is complete in all respects. When men attempt to denigrate them, women shouldn't fall apart; they should never believe they are inferior to men. It is women who have given birth to every single man in this world. Take pride in this unique blessing and move forward with faith in your inherent

Introduction

power. You should never think of yourself as a weak little lamb, but always as a lioness."

When Amma finished, she was asked to meet with a group of about 30 "young leaders" from countries throughout the world, including many lands currently involved in some form of conflict. These included Afghanistan, Iraq, Iran, Pakistan, India, Sri Lanka, Tibet, Nepal, Cambodia, Laos,

During the summit, Amma met with a group of about 30 "young leaders" from countries throughout the world, including many lands currently involved in some form of conflict. These included Afghanistan, Iraq, Iran, Pakistan, India, Sri Lanka, Tibet, Nepal, Cambodia, Laos, Taiwan, South Africa, Nigeria, Mexico, Israel and Palestine.

The Infinite Potential of Women

Taiwan, South Africa, Nigeria, Mexico, Israel and Palestine.

It was at that time that the Initiative's chairwoman, Reverend Dr. Joan Brown Campbell, a former executive director of the U.S. Office of the World Council of Churches, approached Amma with a request: "Amma, we have a dream that one of the results of this meeting will be the creating of a council of women spiritual leaders from around the world. Our hope is that if we form such a council that we might be able to be a place where people can come when they look for a word from women, a word of wisdom. And you certainly could be the person who could most give us that wisdom. Will you, Amma, be willing to play a leading role in this council? If you would be willing to stand with us, we would be honoured." With utmost humility, Amma agreed, saying that she would certainly do what she could.

Reverend Brown and Dena Merriam, the Initiative's founder and convener, then introduced to Amma the various young people. Looking deeply at each of them, Amma praised their precocious spiritual inclinations and desire to dedicate them-

Introduction

selves to the fostering of peace. "At such a young age these youngsters have awoken and developed spiritual awareness. Such a thing is amazing in itself and worth our praise," Amma said.

Amma then suggested that the Initiative allow the youth to play a role in the newly forming council. "If they could hold the reins, it will help all the nations," Amma said. "If they join together, they will become like a beautiful rainbow."

Stressing the importance of action over words, Amma extolled the virtues of youth. "The youth have the energy to actually roll up their sleeves and run around and do things," Amma said with a smile. "You just have to guide them and share your experiences with them, and they can take up the leadership. We should also support them emotionally, intellectually and give them the necessary instructions at the right time. Particularly in the conflict areas people are really looking forward to some guidance. What we really need is not physical meetings, but meetings of hearts. We should *do* something. That is what is needed."

Amma then advised the youth and Initiative leaders to remember that human effort alone is not enough, that without divine grace no plans come to fruition. "Become humble," Amma said. "Remain a beginner till the end, like a child endowed with tremendous faith and patience. That is the best path. Such should be our attitude towards life and the experiences life brings to us. Then we will keep on learning. Our bodies have grown in all directions but not the mind. For the mind to grow and become as big as the universe, we should become a child.

"So, move forward. Go to your respected areas, feel the suffering of the people and work hard. There is a lot to learn. Let us do what we can do. May God's grace bless us all."

Amma's vision regarding the role of women in various areas of life, including politics and governmental administration, shows her universal perspective—a vision born out of her inner realization of unity and peace. According to Amma, empowering women doesn't mean rebuffing men and settling old scores with them. On the contrary, Amma's is a vision of forgiveness, mutual understanding and love. Only action based on

Introduction

such an expansive vision can carry humankind to both spiritual and material heights.

Swami Amritaswarupananda Puri
Vice-Chairman
Mata Amritanandamayi Math

The Infinite Potential of Women

An Address by Sri Mata Amritanandamayi Devi

Jaipur, Rajasthan, India — March 7th 2008

All around the world, heated discussions are arising about giving women an equal place to men in all spheres of society, according them the same respect and reverence. This is a welcome sign of change. Women have had to silently suffer for a long time without such dialogue. Throughout history, women have been subject to physical, emotional and intellectual exploitation and persecution. Even in countries where there is supposed to be progressive thinking and development, women are still being discriminated against in many arenas, even though its intensity has somewhat decreased. Changing times have compelled men to grant women physical protection, but even today, men are reluctant to allow women an environment free of intellectual and emotional inequality and pressure—whether at work, home or in society. As long as this attitude remains, a shadow will continue to loom over the relations between women and men and also over society as a whole. Without mutual respect and loving acknowledgment, the lives of women and men will be like two distant shores without a bridge to connect them. If woman is to relate to man and man to woman, both must cultivate greater understanding, mental maturity and intellectual discrimination. If these are absent, discordant notes, arrhythmic patterns and unrest will be the hallmarks of society. Equality must be created in the mind. Presently, our minds are being ruled by notions of inequality. As long as this prevails, society's growth and development will remain incomplete, like a half-blossomed flower. Alienating women from matters of finance and politics is to discard half the intellect and strength of society. Men must become aware of the progress society and the individual can make if women are sincerely invited to co-operate in such matters. Without doubt, forums, think-tanks and publicity campaigns are necessary to bring about a solution to this problem. However, thinking in purely intellectual terms will not rectify the situation. We need to uncover its gross and subtle causes to arrive at a solution.

Women say that they are not being given the status, consideration and freedom they deserve at home, at work or in society. They say, not only are they not respected, they are even treated with contempt. Men do not like hearing this truth. They feel women are being given too much freedom as is and have become arrogant, neglecting their homes and children. Before considering what aspects of these perspectives are right and what are wrong, we need to understand how this situation arose and trace its roots. If we can do this, it will be easier to change misconceptions.

In the past, the condescending notion, "Man is superior to woman. She does not need freedom or an equal place," became entrenched in the minds of most men. The mentality of women, however, is altogether different. They feel: "For so long, men have lorded over and exploited us. We've had enough! From now on, we need to teach them a lesson; there's no other way."

The Infinite Potential of Women

Both these stances are fraught with resentment and enmity. Today, such destructive thoughts control both women and men, inflating egos and further confounding the problem. For our minds to be free, we must abandon this competitive mentality of "Who is better?"

Once, there was a wedding. After the wedding, when the husband and wife had to formalize the marriage by signing the marriage register, the husband signed his name first. Then it was the wife's turn. As soon as she finished signing, the husband shouted, "It's over… it's all over! I want a divorce at once!"

The magistrate and the others present were stunned. The magistrate asked, "Hey, what's this all about? You want a divorce just after getting married? What happened?"

The groom said, "What *happened*? Just open your eyes and look! There, look at my signature. Now look at hers! See how huge it is? Tell me, does anyone sign over the whole page? I understand what this means. I'm not a fool. In life, she will be big and I will be small. This is what she means. Well, forget that! She is not going to belittle me!"

Today when men and women attempt to walk hand-in-hand, their steps falter right from the start.

Women are questioning socially fabricated rules and regulations and starting to awaken and advance. But due to habitual attitudes and traditions, men are not allowing them to awaken.

"We have, in fact, given women freedom," say the men. But of what sort?

A man gave a friend a precious gem. But the moment he gave it away, he started lamenting, "What a pity! I shouldn't have given it away." He continued to grieve and brood over what he had done. Not only that, he then started to scheme of ways to get it back. Similar is the spirit with which men have granted women their freedom. In fact, freedom is not something for men to grant women; it is her birthright. Men snatched it away and made it their own.

In the past, men had the freedom and license to do anything, as they were the only ones working. Because control over the finances and other matters were in their hands, they exercised an authority that imprisoned women. Then they went about their affairs holding the key in their hands. But now the situation has changed. Even if locked in, women are opening the doors from the inside and breaking free. The reason is: today, women are educated, have jobs and the means to stand on their own two feet. Men must understand times have changed.

Before, women were confined within the cages of socially created regulations. They had to observe the dogmas passed down through generations while living in obedience. "Respect men," "Ask no question," "Do as you're told"—such rules were enforced upon women. Because of this oppression, they were unable to express their talents. A potted plant like a bonsai will not bear flowers or fruit. Isn't it merely a decorative object? Similarly, women were seen only as objects for men's pleasure and happiness. She was like a *tambura*, strummed only to accompany the song of man.

Once, a reporter visited a foreign country to research a story. In the city, he noticed a group of people moving through the streets. The men walked in front, while the women followed in the rear, carrying their children in their arms and heavy loads on their shoulders. Wherever he travelled in that country, the reporter saw the same sight. He thought, "This is terrible. Are the men here so old-fashioned?"

After a few months, war broke out in that country. In order to understand the post-war conditions, the reporter revisited the country. This time, he saw just the opposite. Now the women were in the front and the men at the back, bearing both the children and the loads. The reporter rejoiced, thinking, "What an amazing change the war has brought about!" He asked one of the women about this change. As he did so, he heard an explosion. One of the women had stepped on a landmine and was instantly killed. The woman being interviewed said, "See the *change*? This is just a new scheme the men have devised to protect themselves!"

This is only an example. May such a situation never come to pass. Everyone thinks only of his own safety. Men should be happy. But let it not be at the expense of the happiness of women.

In some countries, people even used to believe that women did not have souls. If a man killed his wife in such a country, he would not be punished. After all, how could killing someone without a soul be considered a crime?

"Women are weak. They need men to protect them." This has been the prevailing thought for generations. Society has assigned man the role of protector. But men have used this role to exploit women. In fact, men should neither position themselves as the protector nor punisher of women. They should co-exist with women, with the readiness and open-mindedness to allow women into the vanguard of mainstream society.

Many people ask: how did this male ego come? According to Vedanta [the philosophy of non-duality], the ultimate cause may be *maya* [illusion], but on a more basic level there could be another source. In ancient times, humans lived in forests, staying in caves or tree houses. Because men are physically stronger than women, it was they who did the hunting and protected the families from wild animals. Women mainly would stay at home, looking after the children and doing household chores. As it was the men who brought home the food and the skins used to make clothing, they may have developed the idea that women were dependent on them for survival—that they were the masters and women were the servants. In this way, women also may have begun to look at men as their protectors. This might be how such egos developed.

Woman is not weak and should never be considered so, but her natural compassion and sympathy have too often been misinterpreted as weaknesses. If a woman draws on her power within, she can become more of a man than a man[1]. Male society should sincerely help her realize and acknowledge her latent strength. If we align ourselves with that inner strength, this world can become a heaven. War, strife and terrorism will come to an end. Needless to say, love and compassion will become part and parcel of life.

Amma has heard of an incident regarding a war in an African country. Countless men died in this war. Although women made up 70 per-

---

[1] In India, virtues associated with men include courage, discrimination and detachment. Female virtues include love, compassion and patience.

cent of the population, they did not lose courage from their loss. They joined together in unity. Individually and in groups, they started small businesses. They raised both their own children and the orphans. Before long, the women found themselves remarkably empowered and their overall situation radically improved. This proves that, if they so choose, women can rebound from destruction and become a force to be reckoned with.

Due to incidents like this, people conclude, "If a woman rules, many riots and wars can be avoided. After all, a woman would only admit her own children into the killing fields after careful consideration. Only a mother can understand the pain of another who has lost her child."

If women unite and stand together, they can bring about many desirable changes in society. But men also need to encourage them to come together. Women and men should join hands to save our society and the coming generations from a huge disaster—this is what Amma has to say. Instead, the situation today is akin to two heavily loaded vehicles speeding towards each other from opposite directions, each unprepared to move aside to let the other pass.

There are differences in the outlook, approach and activities of men and women according to differences in time, place and culture. Nevertheless, courageous women have lived in every age and broken out from the cages that were imposed on them to start revolutions. Indian princesses like Rani Padmini, Hathi Rani, Mirabai and Jhansi Rani were such symbols of valour and purity.

Similar jewels of womanhood have existed in other countries too. Some examples are Florence Nightingale, Joan of Arc and Harriet Tubman. Whenever opportunities have presented themselves, women have outshone men in every field. A woman has the talent and strength to do so.

There is invincible strength in woman. If she can escape the utterly dark prison cell of her mind and emotions, she can soar into the endless skies of freedom.

Once, by chance, a baby eagle found itself living amongst a brood of chicks. The mother hen raised it in the same way she raised her own offspring. Like the chicks, the young eagle grew up foraging the ground for worms. As such, the eagle thought itself to be a mere chicken, ignorant of its ability to fly and soar into the air. One day, another eagle noticed this eagle fledgling with the chicks. When it was alone, the 'sky eagle' approached the 'chicken eagle' and brought it to a lake. The 'sky eagle' said, "My child, don't you know who you are? Here, look at me and now look at your own reflection in the water. Like me, you too are an eagle with the ability to soar in the sky—not an earth-bound chicken." Gradually the eagle realized its strength, and then, without much delay, spread its wings and soared into the sky.

The vast sky is the eagle's birthright. In the same way, a woman has the potential to soar into the endless sky of strength and freedom. But before this freedom can become a reality, woman must prepare herself through steady effort. It is the thought that she is powerless and saddled by numerous limitations and weaknesses that inhibits her. She must first eliminate such thinking. Then a change will spontaneously occur within. However, she should not mistake the freedom of the Inner Self to be that of the body.

Still, Amma would say that women should give up their tendency of finding fault with men. Men need the physical and emotional support of women. In general, it is true that men do not think highly of women. However, they cannot be completely blamed. The age-old traditions and situations in which they've been raised have instilled this outlook within them. For example, if an American comes to India and is told to give up his fork and knife to eat with his hand, he may not be able to do so immediately. Similar is the case with a person's habitual nature; one may not be able to change it so quickly. Expecting men to change immediately is just as unreasonable. They are being led by a mind that is unknown to them. If someone falls in front of an elephant, the elephant will raise its leg to step on him. Even a baby elephant will do this. Such is the power of ingrained nature. Instead of blaming men, we should patiently and lovingly strive to change them gradually.

If we try to force open the petals of a flower while it is still a bud, its beauty and fragrance will be lost. We must allow the flower to blossom

The Infinite Potential of Women

naturally. Similarly, condemning men or demanding that they change quickly and pressuring them will adversely affect the family and social life of both women and men. Therefore, men should understand the mental predisposition of women and vice versa.

"We must forge ahead." This is the focus of most women. It's true, women must move forward, but they also need to turn back to consider the child following in their footsteps, not discarding their parental responsibilities. For the sake of her children, a mother should have at least some patience. It is not enough to give a baby space in her womb, she must also give it space in her heart.

The integrity, beauty and fragrance of future society should be expressed through mothers. The mother is the first teacher. As such, she is the one who can influence a child the most. Whatever the mother does, the child will imbibe. A mother's breast milk does more than nourish just the baby's body. It also develops the baby's mind, intellect and heart. Similarly, the life values a mother transmits to her child give it strength and courage in the future. Since women have given birth to and raised men, how can women not be equal to them? Only if mothers awaken and put forth effort is a new era filled with love, compassion and prosperity possible.

A long time ago, a pregnant queen summoned her astrologer when her labour pains began. He predicted, "The time beginning a few hours from now is the most auspicious for giving birth. If the child is born then, you will give birth to a boy who will be the embodiment of all noble qualities. He will be a blessing to the country and to the people." When she heard this, the queen had her legs tied to the ceiling, with her head hanging down, hands touching the ground. In order to know when the favourable time arrived, she placed a clock nearby. When the time drew near, she instructed her friends to prepare her for the delivery. She gave birth at exactly the auspicious time mentioned. Due to the trauma she wilfully incurred to bring about the fortunate birth, the queen died. Later, when her son became king, he worked tirelessly for the good of the people and the country. He constructed innumerable temples that were objects of great beauty. The land flourished and the people were peaceful, content and happy.

Today, people think only of what they can get. We should not think in terms of what we can get, but more in terms of what we can give for the good of society.

The inner strength of women flows like a river. If the current of a river encounters a mountain, the river will flow around it. If there is a cluster of rocks, the river will flow through them. Sometimes, it may flow under or over them. Similarly, feminine strength has the capacity to move toward the goal, overcoming any obstacle it encounters. Men must be ready to give the inner strength of women the value it deserves. For the sake of society's collective growth, men should accept and encourage women with an open mind.

In the past, men were like single-lane, one-way roads. Now, they need to become like highways. Not only should they make it convenient for women to move ahead, they must also give way to them. Men may have more muscle and physical strength than women, but instead of using this strength to suppress women, they can use it to support them. Organizations should hold meetings aimed at giving leadership positions to women as well. But we should remember that equality is not a matter of power or position. It is a mental state.

Women and men should honour the heart with the same importance they are giving to the intellect. They should strive to work in a way that reconciles intellect and heart, and be role models for each other. Then, equality and harmony will come about naturally. Equality is not something external. A hen can never crow like a rooster. But can a rooster lay eggs? Even if there are external differences, it is possible to become of one mind. Electricity manifests in a refrigerator as coldness, in a heater as warmth and in a bulb as light. A television will not have the same qualities as a light bulb, nor a light bulb that of a television. Nor will a refrigerator be able to do what the heater does, and vice versa. However, the electric current that flows through all these appliances is one and the same. Likewise, although there may be external differences between women and men, the indwelling consciousness is one.

The Infinite Potential of Women

Everything has its place in the universe; nothing is insignificant. There is a significance and consciousness behind each expression of creation. Everything has its own essential nature; some things may be "big," others "small." Light is the nature of the sun, waves the nature of the sea and coolness the nature of wind. What endows a deer with placidity and a lion with cruelty is its own original nature. Similarly, women and men have their own unique natures that distinguish them from each other. These should be remembered and never abandoned.

In their attempt to defeat men, some women now smoke and drink like them, forgetting their gift of motherhood. Doing so is not only dangerous; it simply will not bring about the sought-after changes.

Man is not better than woman, nor is woman better than man. The fundamental truth is that in creation, no one is superior to anyone else. Attributing supremacy to God alone, women and men can become instruments in the service of the Almighty. It is from this approach that true equality between them can emerge.

What we are seeing today is a clash between past and future. The male community that stands unwilling to compromise is the emblem of the past. If the future is to be a beautiful, fragrant, fully blossomed flower, women and men must join hands in all spheres. Those who desire peace and contentment in the world community must pay heed to this, right now, in this very moment. For the sake of a promising future, the minds and intellects of women and men need to become one. We cannot wait any longer. The more we delay, the worse the state of affairs in the world will become.

If women and men unite, they can establish healthy governance. But in order for this shift to come about, there needs to be mutual understanding and open-hearted dialogue. Snake venom can cause death. But it can also be converted into medicine capable of saving someone's life. Likewise, if we can convert our negative thoughts into abilities, we can still save society. Only love can transform the venom of negative thoughts into ambrosia.

Love is an emotion common to all living

beings. It is the path women can take to reach men, men to women, both to Nature, and Nature to the universe. And the love that overflows all boundaries is *vishwa matrutvam*—universal motherhood.

The greatest flowering that can take place on this earth is that of the flower of love. A beautiful flower with colour and fragrance blossoms naturally, even from a small plant. In a similar way, love sprouts in human hearts, then blossoms and expands. Both women and men should permit this flowering from within.

There is nothing more profound than the strength and beauty of two hearts that love each other. Love has the mind-cooling freshness of the full moon and the scintillating brilliance of the sun's rays. But love will not enter our hearts without permission. Women and men should be equally willing to invite within this love that is waiting. Only love can bring about a permanent change in the mind-sets and, therefore, the realities of women and men.

If the wife and husband live in mutual understanding, the increasing sense of alienation between them will decrease. In this way, the problems in society will also be reduced to a certain extent. Today, a wife and husband may even proclaim, just to delude others: "We are living together in mutual love and faith." This is make-believe love. Love is not something to be imagined or faked, but lived. It is life itself.

Pretending is like wearing a mask. No matter who dons it, it must be removed. Otherwise, time will remove it. Depending on the duration of the character's role, some will remove it earlier, whereas others may have it removed from them a little later. This is the only difference.

How did love, which is the intrinsic nature and obligation of a human being, become a mask? It is when one denigrates oneself by acting without humility or compromise that love becomes a pretence. For example, if you just stand by a clear river and look, will your thirst be quenched? In order to quench one's thirst, one must bend down to drink the water. Instead of doing this, if one remains standing upright and curses the river, what is the point? It is just as easy to fill ourselves with the crystalline waters of love, if we surrender.

Women and men in relationships today have become like secret police. Whatever they see or hear makes them suspicious. Such doubt robs them of longevity and health, and is indeed a serious disease. People afflicted with this disease lose their capacity to listen empathetically to the problems of each other.

Even though many relationships are suffering, we have not lost love forever. If love dies, the universe will die. The undying ember of love is in everyone. We simply need to blow on it and it will be fanned into flames.

We are seeing more and more species of animals becoming extinct. Are we going to allow love to become extinct in the human heart in the same way? To prevent this extinction of love itself, human beings must return to respecting, worshiping and reposing their faith in a divine power. That power is not outside. But in order to discover it inside, we need to adjust our perspective. For example, while reading a book, what we focus on are only the words, not the paper on which the words have been neatly printed. The paper is the substratum on which the words have been made clear.

Try this experiment with a few people. Cover a fairly big board with white paper. Make a small black mark in the centre of the white paper. Then ask those present, "What do you see?" Most people will probably say, "I see a small black dot." Very few will say, "I see a black mark in the centre of a large piece of white paper."

Humanity today is like this. We must first recognize that love is the very nucleus of life. When we read, we must certainly be able to see the letters. However, when reading, we must also acknowledge the paper that is the substratum. Today, instead of looking outward from the inside, we are trying to look inward from the outside. In this way, we will not be able to see anything clearly.

In worldly life, women and men have their own needs and rights while vying to gain money, position, prestige and freedom. Striving hard to gain all these, they are expending so much time and effort. Amidst all this exertion, we should set aside a corner of our mind to remember one truth: Without love, we will not be able to derive happiness or satisfaction from any name, fame, position or money. Our mind, intellect and body need to be resolutely fixed on pure love, which is the centre-point of life. It is vital to work from this centre of pure love. Then the differences between women and men will only manifest in the realm of form and we will realize that, in essence, we are one.

Jaipur is an ideal place for this conference. The earth here has borne witness to a noble culture. Princesses of uncommon valour and unworldly purity were born and lived here. Through their pure minds and powerful sacrifices, they upheld invaluable ideals in life. Courage and mental purity are qualities a woman needs, regardless of time or place. If these qualities become her very life-breath, society will place her on a pedestal, and the position, name, fame and adoration she deserves will reach her spontaneously.

Actually, mental purity is the basis of courage, and the source of mental purity is love. Only love can liberate women and men from the dark prisons of the past and usher them into the light of truth. Love and freedom are interdependent. Love can only dawn in a heart that has been freed from thoughts of the past. Only when there is love within will the mind become free. When the mind becomes free, one attains complete freedom in life.

If we want to gain freedom, equality and happiness, human beings must either love one another or love Nature. Or else, they must strive to realize their Inner Self. The time for doing any one of these is long overdue. Further delay at this point spells grave danger for humanity.

Many women come to Amma crying and ask: "Why did God have to make us women?" When Amma asks them why they would ask such a thing, they say, "Men are harassing us physically and mentally. When they speak it is full of condescension. Because of this we are beginning to feel disgusted with ourselves." They feel that to be born a woman is a curse, and that to be born a man is superior in every way. Under the weight of their inferiority complex, they find themselves without the strength to stand up to others. Perhaps it is such thoughts and experiences that lead women to commit female infanticide. The thought of subjecting yet another woman to such a cruel world fills them with fear.

Dowry has long been illegal, but that fact hasn't reduced the sums being given and received in marriages.

How can we end this custom of dowry, which reinforces the idea of women as second-rate and defective in comparison to men? How can poor families who have to struggle just to get proper clothing ever hope to raise enough money for dowry? There are women who kill their newborn daughters for this reason alone.

Frankly, in India divorce laws do not favour women. Once the cases come to court, they become veritable wars. Even today, huge delays cause divorce cases to drag on for years. And at the end of it all the woman rarely sees more than 400 or 500 rupees a month. After the divorce, women who have had children are forced to support them independently. The paltry sum they are awarded is barely enough to feed them for a week. As a result some women have no choice but to turn to prostitution. Amma herself has dried the tears of many women who are forced to lead double lives, alternating weeks at home and weeks at the brothels. Others try to get jobs as maidservants. But there they often suffer unspeakable abuse at the hands of their employers, who swoop down like vultures to feast upon their helpless bodies. Ultimately, they too turn to prostitution. Their children then follow in their footsteps. At a very young age, they are also taken in by the brothels. And soon they are coerced into conceiving. Their overlords then hold these young women hostage with the threat, "Should you leave, you will never see your child again." In this way they are forced to continue.

In the West, prostitutes are more aware of the potential consequences of their actions and take the necessary precautions. But in India these women fall victim to countless sexual diseases, turning their existence into living hells. This entire cycle begins with man's lack of respect for women and the inferiority complexes generated as a result.

Another problem we see today is that incidences of rape are ever increasing. Some say the reason is the provocative way in which women are dressing in the modern world. But this is not completely true because in olden days, in some sections of society, women in India did not wear blouses. They covered themselves with only a single cloth. To see such woman even wearing a proper shawl was uncommon. Nevertheless, in those days rape was rarely heard of. Why? Because spiritual values had a strong influence on day-to-day life and people had an awareness of *dharma*—conducting one's self with respect and care for humanity as a whole. Due to traffic lights and radar cameras, people are forced to observe speed limits. They know if they are caught speeding too many times they will lose their license. In the same way, long ago, even a starving man would not steal due to his deeply ingrained values. Even though men were attracted to women, they maintained self-control. Their awareness of *dharma* and their resultant fear kept them in line.

Advancements in Information Technology have greatly benefited society. But because people use the Internet and television without proper discrimination, they have become another instigator of rape and deviant behaviour. Anyone can access inappropriate websites. They awaken animalistic tendencies in people. Many Gulf countries have implemented strict measures to block access to such sites. India should also consider implementing similar measures. Some people may say, "Everyone is free!", "Choice is our birthright!" or "It's all part of modern education!" But if we refrain from introducing such restrictions in order to placate such arguments, our future generations will be destroyed. The blood will be on our hands.

In life, *artha* and *kama*—the gathering of money and the fulfilling of desires—are not enough; first and foremost there must be awareness of *dharma*—righteousness.

Before concluding, Amma would like to make a few suggestions that she feels could offer women some relief from the suffering they are currently experiencing in society:

1. Female infanticide is punishable by law, but these laws are not being enforced. The government

must take the necessary steps to ensure people who violate such laws are brought to justice.

2. Women with know-how, education and financial wealth should help uplift women who are uneducated and financially impoverished. However, all such efforts should give importance to values and culture, and never serve as a means to question the belief or faith of villagers.

3. In order to bring about equality between women and men, it is critical for women to become financially independent. For this, education is necessary. Parents should pledge to ensure that their daughters are educated as much as possible and thus help them to be capable of standing on their own two feet. As age is no barrier to education, women should get together to come up with creative ways to educate illiterate women.

4. Every time a female child is born, it would be good if the government were to put aside some money in her name. In this way, by the time the girl is of marrying age, she will have the necessary funds. This would reduce female infanticide.

5. It would be nice if more institutions were started in order to take in unwanted female infants. One such organization is called "Mother's Cradle." Awareness of such organizations should be increased in society.

6. At any time of night, women should be able to walk alone without fear. Men should put forth sincere effort to see that this becomes a reality.

7. In Sanskrit, the word for "dowry" is *stri dhanam*. Stri means 'woman'; dhanam means 'wealth.' Men who light up with greed when thinking about dowry should realize that stri *is* dhanam—women *are* the wealth gained in marriage.

8. As important as it is to provide girls with quality education, it is equally important to hold awareness campaigns for boys. While still young, they must come to comprehend, in all its depth, that a woman is not a tradable commodity, nor a ball to be kicked around by a man. She is Mother, worthy of respect and worship.

9. In India, the divorce rate is on the rise. In the west when a couple divorces, the man usually has to pay alimony until the woman remarries. But in India, such systems are not enforced. This should be rectified.

10. Women should also strive to draw men into efforts to bring about equality between women and men.

11. To a certain extent, male society has succeeded in promoting the fallacy that "Women do not have strength or courage." It is time to prove this belief wrong, though not by challenging anyone or by competing with men. Through the pure essence of motherhood inherent in all women, which is afraid not even of death, and through an unshakeable self-confidence that prepares her for giving birth to new creation, woman constantly shows the world that she *is* strength and the very epitome of courage.

If you tell a person who holds a PhD, "You don't have a PhD!", will it in any way invalidate his degree? No. Likewise, women already hold everything they need to shine forth in society. She is faultless. She is complete in all respects. When men attempt to denigrate them, women shouldn't fall apart; they should never believe they are inferior to men. It is women who have given birth to every single man in this world. Take pride in this unique blessing and move forward with faith in your inherent power. You should never think of yourself as a weak little lamb, but always as a lioness.

The external eyes and ears of human beings, saturated by selfishness and egoism, are always open. However, the inner eyes needed to see the sorrows of others and the inner ears needed to compassionately hear stories of the suffering remain closed. It is Amma's heartfelt prayer that this heartbreaking condition be rapidly transformed. May we all listen to, care about and respond to the problems of others. May everyone pray for the happiness and peace of others. Amma offers these prayers to the Paramatma—the Supreme Self.

||Om Lokah Samastah Sukhino Bhavantu||

Book Catalog
By Author

Sri Mata Amritanandamayi Devi
108 Quotes On Faith
108 Quotes On Love
Compassion, The Only Way To Peace: Paris Speech
Cultivating Strength And Vitality
Living In Harmony
May Peace And Happiness Prevail: Barcelona Speech
May Your Hearts Blossom: Chicago Speech
Practice Spiritual Values And Save The World: Delhi Speech
The Awakening Of Universal Motherhood: Geneva Speech
The Eternal Truth
The Infinite Potential Of Women: Jaipur Speech
Understanding And Collaboration Between Religions
Unity Is Peace: Interfaith Speech

Swami Amritaswarupananda Puri
Ammachi: A Biography
Awaken Children, Volumes 1-9
From Amma's Heart
Mother Of Sweet Bliss
The Color Of Rainbow

Swami Jnanamritananda Puri
Eternal Wisdom, Volumes 1-2

Swami Paramatmananda Puri
On The Road To Freedom Volumes 1-2
Talks, Volumes 1-6

Swami Purnamritananda Puri
Unforgettable Memories

Swami Ramakrishnananda Puri
Eye Of Wisdom
Racing Along The Razor's Edge
Secret Of Inner Peace
The Blessed Life
The Timeless Path
Ultimate Success

Swamini Krishnamrita Prana
Love Is The Answer
Sacred Journey
The Fragrance Of Pure Love
Torrential Love

M.A. Center Publications
1,000 Names Commentary
Archana Book (Large)
Archana Book (Small)
Being With Amma
Bhagavad Gita
Bhajanamritam, Volumes 1-6
Embracing The World
For My Children
Immortal Light
Lead Us To Purity
Lead Us To The Light
Man And Nature
My First Darshan
Puja: The Process Of Ritualistic Worship
Sri Lalitha Trishati Stotram

Amma's Websites

AMRITAPURI—Amma's Home Page
Teachings, Activities, Ashram Life, eServices, Yatra, Blogs and News
http://www.amritapuri.org

AMMA (Mata Amritanandamayi)
About Amma, Meeting Amma, Global Charities, Groups and Activities and Teachings
http://www.amma.org

EMBRACING THE WORLD®
Basic Needs, Emergencies, Environment, Research and News
http://www.embracingtheworld.org

AMRITA UNIVERSITY
About, Admissions, Campuses, Academics, Research, Global and News
http://www.amrita.edu

THE AMMA SHOP—Embracing the World® Books & Gifts Shop
Blog, Books, Complete Body, Home & Gifts, Jewelry, Music and Worship
http://www.theammashop.org

IAM—Integrated Amrita Meditation Technique®
Meditation Taught Free of Charge to the Public, Students, Prisoners and Military
http://www.amma.org/groups/north-america/projects/iam-meditation-classes

AMRITA PUJA
Types and Benefits of Pujas, Brahmasthanam Temple, Astrology Readings, Ordering Pujas
http://www.amritapuja.org

GREENFRIENDS
Growing Plants, Building Sustainable Environments, Education and Community Building
http://www.amma.org/groups/north-america/projects/green-friends

FACEBOOK
This is the Official Facebook Page to Connect with Amma
https://www.facebook.com/MataAmritanandamayi

DONATION PAGE
Please Help Support Amma's Charities Here:
http://www.amma.org/donations